IN SEARCH OF
DINOSAURS

Written and illustrated by Tony Gibbons

Contents

British Library Cataloguing in Publication Data
Gibbons, Tony
In search of dinosaurs
1. Dinosaurs
I. Title
567.91
ISBN 0–7498–0195–6

Created and illustrated by Tony Gibbons
courtesy of Bernard Thornton Artists, London.
Copyright © 1991 World International Publishing Limited.
All rights reserved.
Published in Great Britain by World International Publishing Limited,
An Egmont Company, Egmont House,
P.O. Box 111, Great Ducie Street,
Manchester M60 3BL.
Printed in Belgium.

WORLD INTERNATIONAL PUBLISHING LIMITED
MANCHESTER

MAN
HUMAN LIFE
TERTIARY
PLEISTOCENE
CRETACEOUS

JURASSIC

TRIASSIC

PERMIAN

CARBONIFEROUS

DEVONIAN

SILURIAN

ORDOVICIAN

CAMBRIAN

Dawn of life

The planet Earth is about 4,500 million years old. It was very different then from the planet we live on today. The outer surface was boiling hot. Living creatures could not survive because there was no oxygen in the air. Volcanoes often erupted and thunderstorms shook the sky. It rained and rained for years, creating warm oceans.

The dawn of life on Earth began about 3,500 million years ago. The seas were orange coloured because they were full of chemicals that had washed off the land. The smallest and simplest form of life developed in this orange 'soup' — single cells known as bacteria.

The amount of oxygen increased over millions of years until eventually there was enough to form a screen against the sun's rays. This layer is called ozone and is what makes the sky look blue. Now more advanced forms of life could develop. Among the first forms to appear were simple plants, such as blue-green algae (**1**). In hot weather you can see this algae on the surface of ponds today.

Cells began to group together to make simple plants and animals. Fossil remains of jellyfish (**2**) are dated as being 600 million years old. On the sea-bed there were worms, molluscs, sea-snails and arthropods moving about. Some of these creatures were unlike any alive today.

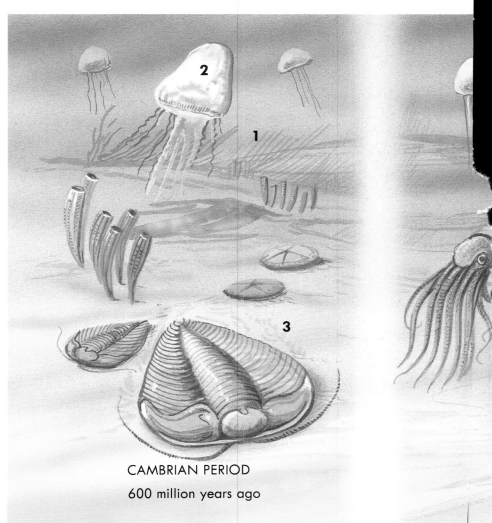

CAMBRIAN PERIOD

600 million years ago

Trilobites (**3**) were arthropods which had a pair of limbs on each segment of their bodies. Trilobites used these limbs for breathing, walking, swimming and handling food. We know about these invertebrates (creatures without backbones) from tracks, tunnels and prints of their bodies left in rocks.

The fossilized remains of sponges have been found in rocks 395 million years old. A living sponge is a fleshy bag held up by a skeleton. It feeds by drawing in water through lots of little holes and removing tiny particles of food.

The cystoid (**4**) had a bunch of limbs at one end and a long body covered with a hard shell. This primitive animal either moved freely through the water or was fixed to rocks by a hollow stalk. The carpoid (**5**) used its single mobile arm to bring food particles to its mouth.

The belemnite (**6**) was possibly one of the first animals to have a layer of flesh. It moved by forcing out jets of water and squirted ink at any attacker. These forms of defence were needed to avoid being eaten by the sea scorpion (**7**).

The major development during the Devonian period was the first appearance of fish. The jawless fish (**8**) had good body armour to save them from being eaten by predators. Cladoselache (**9**) was an early shark. This fierce killer had sharp teeth. It was large compared with the other early forms of life — up to 2 metres (6$\frac{1}{2}$ feet) in length. Cladoselache could swim faster than other fish because it developed a skeleton of cartilage, instead of bone, which is lighter and softer.

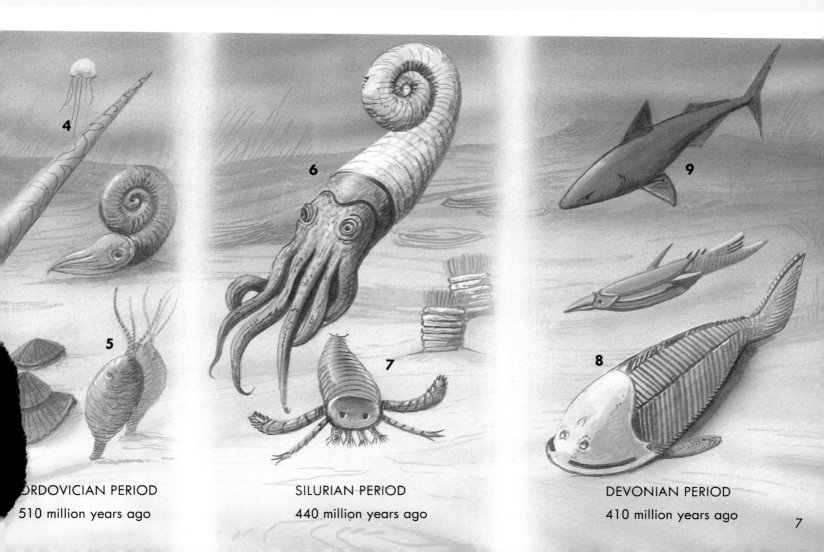

ORDOVICIAN PERIOD
510 million years ago

SILURIAN PERIOD
440 million years ago

DEVONIAN PERIOD
410 million years ago

The first dinosaurs

Where did the first dinosaurs come from? About 380 million years ago, fish with large fins evolved into reptiles. Creatures like **Ichthyostega** and **Diplovertebron** hauled themselves out of the water and crawled short distances over land. They probably returned to the water to breed and feed. **Ichthyostega** swam by waggling its tail. **Diplovertebron** looked like a trotting crocodile. It had five fingers on each limb.

Edaphosaurus was one of the first creatures to lay eggs on land. This meant that land-living animals no longer had to return to water. The flap of skin on its back was like a solar panel. At dawn, **Edaphosaurus** would stand sideways to the sun and soak up the sun's heat. When its blood had warmed up, the animal was able to move about more easily.

Euparkeria first appeared about 225 million years ago. This tiny creature walked on all fours, but reared up on its hind legs when it ran. **Lagosuchus** means 'hare crocodile'. This is a good name for this dinosaur because it had to be a fast runner to catch insects. These early dinosaurs were much smaller than the giants which followed. **Seymouria** hardly ever grew to more than 1 metre ($3\frac{1}{4}$ feet).

True dinosaurs like **Coelophysis** and **Plateosaurus** stood more upright. **Coelophysis** was more dangerous than the very first dinosaurs because it could run faster than other animals. The tall **Plateosaurus** was a plant-eating dinosaur.

Coelophysis *(see-lo-fy-sis)*

primitive fish

Pleuracanthus *(pler-ah-can-thus)*

Ichthyostega *(ik-thee-oh-ste*

Did you know. . .?

A baby **Hypselosaurus** hatched from an egg that was bigger than a rugby football. The baby dinosaur weighed about 1kg (just over 2lb). It grew and grew until it was about 12 metres (40 feet) long and weighed 10 tonnes (9.8 tons). Below: hen's egg (left) and **Hypselosaurus** egg shown to scale.

Plateosaurus *(plat-ee-oh-sor-us)*

Lagosuchus *(lag-oh-sook-us)*

Euparkeria
(yew-park-err-ee-ah)

Edaphosaurus *(ee-daf-oh-sor-us)*

Diplovertebron *(dip-lo-ver-te-bron)*

Seymouria *(see-mor-ee-ah)*

When did dinosaurs roam the Earth?

How old are you? How many years ago were your parents born? Find out how long ago your grandparents were born. That may seem a long time ago to you but think of how long human beings have lived on Earth — about five million years. If you think that is a long time ago, think again. The last dinosaurs roamed the Earth about 65 million years ago. For almost 185 million years before then dinosaurs lived, breathed and ate on the same planet that we live on today.

Ever since the first dinosaur bones were uncovered over 100 years ago, these amazing animals have fascinated people. Every time more dinosaur remains are found, scientists examine them and can tell us more about the lives and times of these animals. There is still a lot we do not know about dinosaurs.

What was a dinosaur? What was life like when these creatures roamed the Earth? Were they as frightening as their size suggests? Why did they die out 65 million years ago? You will have to read on to find the answers to these and other questions.

When the first dinosaurs appeared, the Earth was very different. This is what the Earth was like 225 million years ago. Look in an atlas to see what the Earth is like now. If the land masses were joined up the dinosaurs could roam for thousands of miles looking for food.

Stenonychosaurus
(sten-oh-nike-oh-sor-us)

Struthiomimus
(strooth-ee-oh-mime-us)

Staurikosaurus
(stor-ik-oh-sor-us)

What was a dinosaur?

Dinosaurs were reptiles that lived on Earth. Among them were some of the largest animals that ever lived on land. Some were much longer and taller than any animals alive today. These giants weighed almost as much as a blue whale, about 130 tonnes (128 tons) — yet others were no bigger than a chicken or a rabbit!

The word 'dinosaur' comes from two Greek words — *deinos* meaning 'terrible' and *sauros* meaning 'lizard'. The dinosaurs evolved from reptiles that ran on their hind legs. The first animals to live on land held their legs out sideways to lift their bodies off the ground (see **A**). They looked like crocodiles. The next animals to evolve walked on all fours, but held their bodies higher off the ground (**B**). True dinosaurs had hind legs that went straight down from the body (**C**).

Many dinosaurs developed long hind legs and short front legs. Most of them grasped food with their front legs. They used their strong hind legs for standing and running. The long tail helped the dinosaur to balance when it reached up for food.

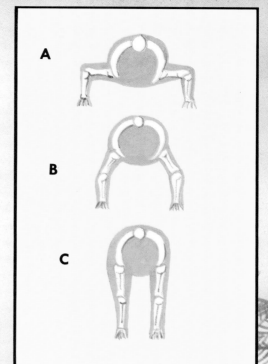

Kuehneosaurus
(koo-een-oh-sor-us)

Saltoposuchus
(sal-toe-po-sook-us)

Massospondylus
(mass-oh-spon-die-lus)

11

Diplodocus

Look at this enormous dinosaur. **Diplodocus** was one of the largest land animals ever to have lived. It had a very long, thin neck and tail. **Diplodocus** was able to reach leaves that were too high for other plant-eaters. Its long tail acted as a balance to stop the dinosaur falling over when it stretched out its neck to feed.

    Diplodocus had to keep its four feet on the ground all of the time. It was a very slow mover. If you watch a large mechanical crane moving slowly round, you will get an idea of the speed at which this giant dinosaur moved. The ground shook as it lumbered along. Although it was too big to run away, **Diplodocus** used its tail like a whip to knock over attackers.

This is an artist's drawing of what the world looked like when **Diplodocus** was roaming the Earth.

Around 150 million years ago, there were more and more animals on the land. Dinosaurs were the rulers of the animal kingdom. The weather was warm and moist.

Look at the two big dinosaurs again.
How did they get enough food through that tiny mouth and down that narrow neck to feed that big body?
It takes lots and lots of food to fill up an animal that size. Perhaps **Diplodocus** never stopped eating!

'Double beam'

Diplodocus gets its name from two Greek words meaning 'double beam'. This giant dinosaur did have two beams. There was one sticking out in front and one at the back — its neck and its tail.

    Diplodocus had a special backbone. Some bones in its tail had a piece which pointed both forward and backwards. Normal backbones only have a piece that points back. That is probably the real reason why **Diplodocus** was given its name.

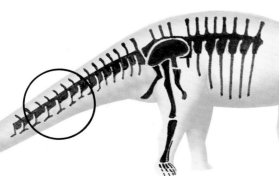

Did you know. . .?

Diplodocus had teeth in the front of its mouth that were like pegs. It used these teeth to comb leaves from twigs. When weak teeth wore down, it is possible that new ones grew in their place.

Brachiosaurus

For many years **Brachiosaurus** was thought to have been the largest dinosaur to have roamed the Earth. (See page 16 for the latest news!) **Brachiosaurus** was certainly a giant monster. Can you imagine a dinosaur that weighed as much as a whole herd of elephants? An adult **Brachiosaurus** weighed about 100 tonnes (98 tons) and was twice as tall as a giraffe. When it moved the earth quaked and the smaller dinosaurs shook!

When **Brachiosaurus** stretched up it could have looked over the roof of a three-storey building. It had no trouble reaching the leaves at tops of trees.

This massive dinosaur had 14 separate bones in its neck. These huge bones had to be strong to support the weight of the dinosaur's long neck. There were hollow spaces in the sides of these neck bones which were full of air. Like **Diplodocus**, this giant dinosaur also had a long tail to balance its long neck.

'Arm lizard'

The name **Brachiosaurus** means 'arm lizard'. It was probably given this name because of its very long front legs. The first **Brachiosaurus** bones were uncovered in 1903. Hundreds of local workers in Tanzania (Africa) dug up the bones by hand. It must have taken several workers to lift a single leg bone. They carried the bones to a port to be shipped to Germany.

This is what the Earth might have looked like 100 million years ago. Look again at the artist's drawing on page 12. Can you see how the continents (land masses) had moved further apart? When the land masses were together, dinosaurs could roam across them for thousands of miles.

Did you know. . .?

nostril

eye

Brachiosaurus had its nostrils on top of its head. An old idea was that this dinosaur lived in deep water, keeping the top of its head out of the water in order to breathe.

It is unlikely that **Brachiosaurus** could stay submerged (under water) for long. The pressure of the water on its rib cage would make breathing difficult. What probably happened was that this giant dinosaur walked out into water to escape from attackers. **Brachiosaurus** could walk out into deeper water than other dinosaurs because its long neck stuck up further and because its nostrils were on the top of its head.

Land of the giants

If you think **Brachiosaurus** was large, then you are in for a big surprise. Some really massive dinosaurs probably lived and breathed all those millions of years ago. The dinosaur bones dug up in Colorado, in the USA, in 1972, were much bigger than the bones of **Brachiosaurus**. This giant of giants has the nickname **'Supersaurus'**. From the few bones that were dug up, scientists have worked out the size and shape of this giant monster. It was 30 metres (100 feet) long and its head was nearly 16.5 metres (54 feet) from the ground.

But wait for it! In 1979, bones belonging to an even bigger dinosaur were found in the same area. These belonged to a creature with the nickname **'Ultrasaurus'**. The bones show that this giant was about 8 metres (26 feet) at the shoulder. That is four times the height of a tall person.

It is possible that an even bigger creature lived in the lands of the giants. Footprints were found in Africa that were made by a beast 48 metres (157 feet) long. So this super dinosaur, called **Breviparopus**, was perhaps the largest animal with a backbone ever to live.

Did you know. . .?

The shoulder blade of the giant monster **'Supersaurus'** is 2.4 metres (8 feet) long.

Brachiosaurus
(brak-ee-oh-sor-us)

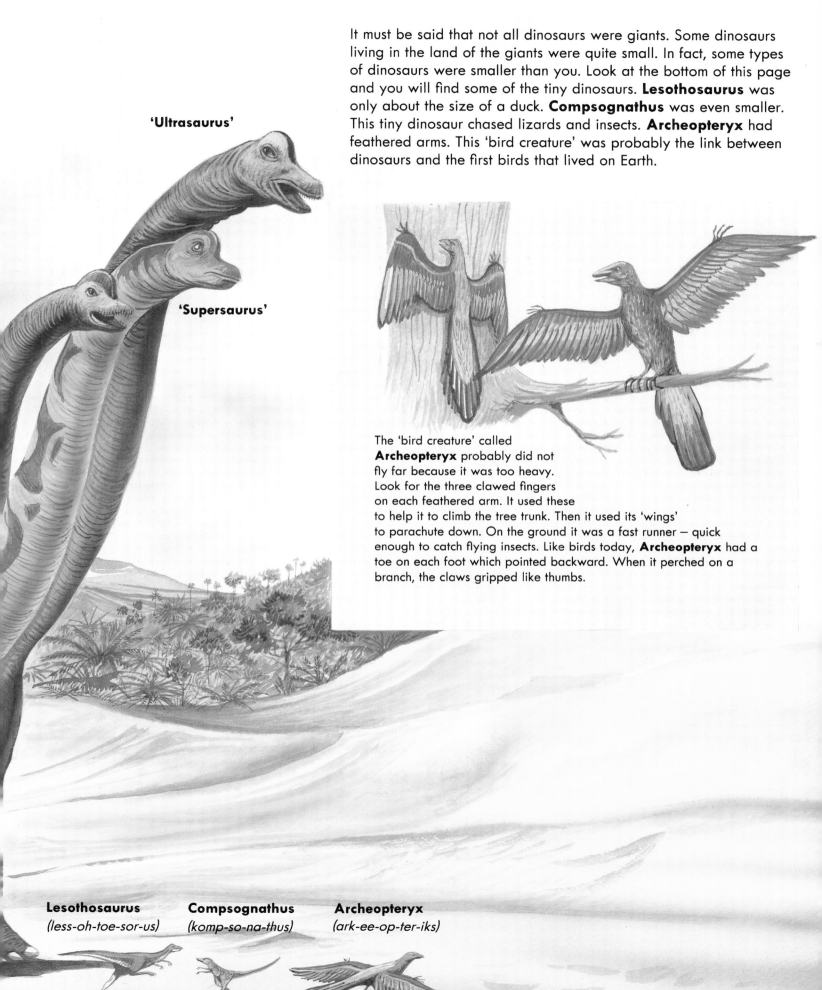

It must be said that not all dinosaurs were giants. Some dinosaurs living in the land of the giants were quite small. In fact, some types of dinosaurs were smaller than you. Look at the bottom of this page and you will find some of the tiny dinosaurs. **Lesothosaurus** was only about the size of a duck. **Compsognathus** was even smaller. This tiny dinosaur chased lizards and insects. **Archeopteryx** had feathered arms. This 'bird creature' was probably the link between dinosaurs and the first birds that lived on Earth.

'Ultrasaurus'

'Supersaurus'

The 'bird creature' called **Archeopteryx** probably did not fly far because it was too heavy. Look for the three clawed fingers on each feathered arm. It used these to help it to climb the tree trunk. Then it used its 'wings' to parachute down. On the ground it was a fast runner — quick enough to catch flying insects. Like birds today, **Archeopteryx** had a toe on each foot which pointed backward. When it perched on a branch, the claws gripped like thumbs.

Lesothosaurus
(less-oh-toe-sor-us)

Compsognathus
(komp-so-na-thus)

Archeopteryx
(ark-ee-op-ter-iks)

17

Plant-eaters

The giant dinosaurs did not charge around fighting and eating each other. In fact, most dinosaurs ate only plants. To help you imagine how much one of these enormous creatures ate in one day, think of the largest animal living on land today, the elephant. An adult African elephant eats up to 200kg (440lb) of plant material each day. A dinosaur such as **Apatosaurus** weighed as much as five elephants so it probably had to eat nearly five times as much food in a day.

Despite the huge size of its body, **Apatosaurus** had a head about the same size as a modern horse. What is more, **Apatosaurus** only had a few front teeth which were the size of large pegs (10cm/4in). These teeth were so weak that it could not tear flesh. Instead, it used its few teeth to comb leaves from trees. It is possible that when the plant-eaters' weak teeth wore down new teeth grew to replace them.

To help churn the food in their stomachs, plant-eating dinosaurs swallowed stones. With the help of strong stomach muscles, the dinosaurs were able to churn the stones and food together. The reason humans do not need to swallow stones is we chew our food first and have stomach juices to do the same work.

Why did many of the plant-eating dinosaurs have such long necks? The answer is the same as for giraffes — they used their long necks to reach leaves high up in trees that other dinosaurs could not reach.

Apatosaurus and **Iguanodon** could rear up on their strong hind legs to feed. **Iguanodon** stripped the leaves off using its long tongue. Then it used the large teeth at the back of its mouth to grind the leaves down.

The dinosaur with the broad snout was a duck-billed dinosaur called **Anatosaurus**. This dinosaur ate trees which grew on hills. If it smelled an approaching attacker, it would blow out the loose skin on its face and make a loud bellowing call to warn others of the danger. Then it would move into nearby water. There were lots of water plants so the plant-eating dinosaurs would not have to stop eating.

Although the plant-eaters could not move quickly, some of them had 'weapons' that they could use in a fight with a meat-eating dinosaur. Look for the **Iguanodon**'s spiky thumbs. It used these like daggers to thrust at its attacker.

Apatosaurus
(a-pat-oh-sor-us)

Iguanodon
(ig-wan-oh-don)

Did you know. . .?

Stones as large as this have been found with dinosaur bones. It is likely that dinosaurs with weak teeth swallowed stones to help grind the plant food to a pulp in their stomachs. Many birds swallow grit and tiny stones to do the same thing.

Anatosaurus
(an-at-oh-sor-us)

Meat-eaters

Let us go back in time to when dinosaurs ruled the animal kingdom on Earth. We arrive in time to see a huge and friendly **Barosaurus** grazing peacefully. Suddenly it is attacked without warning by a group of deadly **Deinonychus**. Although much smaller than their victim they have powerful talons and teeth that make short work of their prey. One of them leaps to attack the giant as others hurry up to join in the fight. They are always able to defeat much larger plant-eating dinosaurs with ease.

The combat rages on as **Barosaurus** tries to whip its powerful tail round to knock over the persistent carnivores. One meat-eater darts away and then turns to come back to the attack. This hungry attacker is **Allosaurus**.

Another deadly enemy of the plant-eaters was **Megalosaurus**. It had large teeth with long roots that held them firmly in the jawbone. These teeth had jagged edges on the front and back, which when used with its strong curved claws, could easily rip the flesh from the body of a dead dinosaur.

Did you know. . .?

About 200 million years ago, the largest meat-eating dinosaur on Earth was probably **Ornithosuchus**. Although it was only 2–3 metres (6–10 feet) long, it was a much heavier version of **Euparkeria** (see page 8). The next meat-eating dinosaurs to appear on Earth were bigger in size than **Ornithosuchus** (see below). Over millions of years, the skins of the dinosaurs became more and more scaly, like the skin of modern lizards.

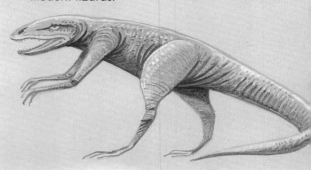

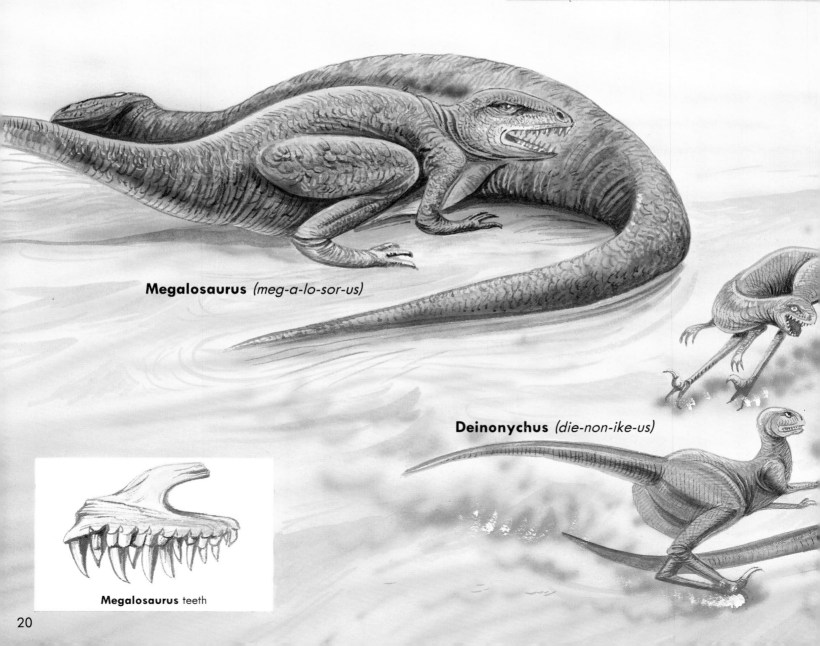

Megalosaurus *(meg-a-lo-sor-us)*

Deinonychus *(die-non-ike-us)*

Megalosaurus teeth

Many meat-eating dinosaurs were able to balance on their hind legs thanks to a long tail that had rod-like bones which strengthened it. This enabled them to run quickly after their prey. **Deinonychus**, which means 'terrible claw', was one such carnivore. It had a large, curved claw on the second toe of each hind leg. The other toes had shorter claws. When it ran, **Deinonychus** flicked the big claw back. Look at the attacker leaping and slashing at its prey. When the giant was killed, **Deinonychus** would balance on one foot so that it could swing the long claw on the other foot to rip open its prey.

Barosaurus *(barrow-sor-us)*

Allosaurus *(al-lo-sor-us)*

Deinonychus claw

'Tyrant lizard'

Tyrannosaurus rex

Here is a hungry meat-eating dinosaur, ready to pounce on a smaller dinosaur.

Tyrannosaurus rex was one of the biggest meat-eating dinosaurs to roam the Earth. It was 15 metres (50 feet) long and was heavier than an adult African elephant which weighs up to 5,900kg (13,000lb).

Its name means 'tyrant lizard', which is a very suitable name for the king of the meat-eaters.

As you can see, **Tyrannosaurus rex** had a long, strong tail and thick hind legs. The sharp claws on its hind legs were like carving knives. But look at its tiny front limbs. These were useless in a fight and too short to lift food to its mouth.

This giant meat-eating dinosaur was not very clever — it had a small brain which dealt mostly with sight and smell. It was not able to do much thinking.

Although **Tyrannosaurus rex** was too big to move quickly, it frightened its prey. It had enormous, sharp teeth and big eyes. What a sight! No wonder the smaller dinosaur, **Scelidosaurus**, looks scared!

When it lumbered over the ground, **Tyrannosaurus rex** growled fiercely and blew bad breath at other dinosaurs. (Perhaps this is where the idea for the dragon came from!)

If **Tyrannosaurus rex** was alive today, it could probably swallow human beings whole!

Did you know. . .?

Tyrannosaurus rex had teeth this size. The zigzag edges helped it to slice through tough skin. A single tooth was as long as 18cm (7in).

Dinosaur defences

The smaller plant-eating dinosaurs were not able to escape the speedy carnivores, so they needed some form of defence. Some grew frills and horns, and others developed bony plates. **Stegosaurus** was a plated dinosaur which lived in swamps in what is now the USA. When the two rows of plates along its back were upright, they were like solar panels. When laid flat, they acted as a form of defence. Sadly, this defence system was not good enough. In time, partly plated dinosaurs which only had their upper parts covered in bony plates and spikes replaced the earlier plated dinosaurs. When attacked, creatures such as **Ankylosaurus** would usually press themselves close to the ground. This protected their soft bellies. **Ankylosaurus** would then swing its bony tail about, clubbing the attacker.

Horned dinosaurs did not evolve until about 70 million years ago. When angry, these plant-eaters charged any attacker, using their sharp horns.

Some dinosaurs were 'head-bangers'. **Pachycephalosaurus** had an extremely thick skull that rose like a dome from the top of its head. This strengthened dome was much thicker than a human skull — up to 20 times thicker. Herds of these dinosaurs roamed the hills in North America and Asia around 100 million years ago. Like many animals today, the males would fight to decide which of them would lead the herd. The noise of blows as their heads clashed could be heard a long way off.

When a herd of plant-eating dinosaurs was attacked, the adults protected their young by forming a ring facing outward. Here you can see a herd of **Triceratops** facing **Tyrannosaurus rex**. The horned dinosaurs used their horns if the attacker got any closer. **Triceratops** had three horns — one on its nose and one over each eye. It also had a bone shield covering its neck.

Kentrosaurus had pairs of long spikes over its back and down its tail. There was also a long spike over each hip. It used its tail spikes as a weapon against any attacker.

The largest of the dinosaurs that had spikes and plates on its back was **Ankylosaurus**. Its main diet was made up of soft plants and insects. The hedgehog of today, with its long, sharp spikes on its back, acts like the **Ankylosaurus** of long ago when threatened.

Pachycephalosaurus means 'thick-headed lizard'. These two males are smashing their heads together in combat but the skulls are so thick that the heads remain undamaged.

Stegosaurus was a plated dinosaur. It also had heavy spikes on its tail. By swinging its tail from side to side it tried to scare away attackers.

Here are two dinosaurs who had bony neck frills as a form of defence. **Anchiceratops** had knobs and spines on its neck frill which pointed backwards. **Chasmosaurus** looked fierce with its spikes and horns.

Death of the dinosaurs

Dinosaurs lived on the Earth for 185 million years. About 65 million years ago the last of them died out. There are three important questions to ask:

- why are there no dinosaurs roaming the Earth today?
- what caused the death of the dinosaurs?
- did they all die at once or did they die out slowly?

Scientists have put forward many ideas about the death of the dinosaurs. The small pictures below show four of these ideas. Experts cannot agree which is right. The only thing they do agree about is that they disagree!

One theory is that a giant meteorite from space crashed into the Earth. This giant ball of red-hot rock, bigger than a mountain, lit the sky with a light brighter than the Sun. It probably set fires raging on the land. If a meteorite this big had hit the Earth it would have made a crater several kilometres wide — but no hole this big has yet been found. Perhaps it landed in the sea and dented the sea-bed. If this did happen then the sea would have flooded the land. If the dinosaurs did not die in the fires on the land, they would now drown.

There is a mystery here. If this is how the dinosaurs died out, why did other animals such as lizards, crocodiles, snakes, and birds survive?

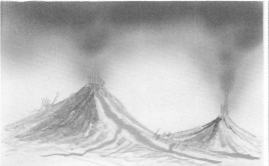

Perhaps many volcanoes erupted at once or perhaps there was a giant earthquake.

Perhaps the weather turned so cold that the dinosaurs froze to death in the permanent winter.

Perhaps egg-thief animals stole all the dinosaur eggs so that no more young dinosaurs were born.

Perhaps a star exploded sending a dust cloud full of radiation down to Earth which killed the dinosaurs.

Discovering dinosaurs today

How do we know about animals that died so many millions of years before there were human beings on Earth? The answer lies under our feet or under the sea. Usually when creatures die their bodies rot and no trace is left. Sometimes the hard parts — like the bones and teeth — are preserved in rock as fossils. The pictures on the right show how this process happens.

This was not the only way. Sometimes the dinosaur bones were buried under desert sands. Sometimes hollows were formed in places where the dinosaur bones used to be. Not all fossil skeletons remained complete. Many of them became scattered for different reasons, such as when corpses were torn into pieces by scavengers or when the land became flooded. Then only a few bones, or sometimes a single bone, will be found. We can still learn a lot from such a find: for example, the size, shape and movements of a dinosaur that lived all those millions of years ago.

At first, dinosaur bones were found by accident. Today we have a better idea of where to start looking. From years of study and experience, experts can now find fossils more easily. Once found, great care is taken not to damage the remains as they are removed for closer study and possible re-assembly at a museum. First, the surrounding rock and earth is removed so that foil or wet tissue paper can be wrapped around the bones. To protect fragile fossils, plaster of Paris or foam is added. Special chemicals are used to harden weak parts of the fossil.

After the bones have been removed, great care is still needed. It can take several years to clean and reconstruct the fossil skeleton for display in a museum. Often, new parts must be made to complete missing portions of the skeleton. Only then can we have a good idea of the dinosaur's appearance.

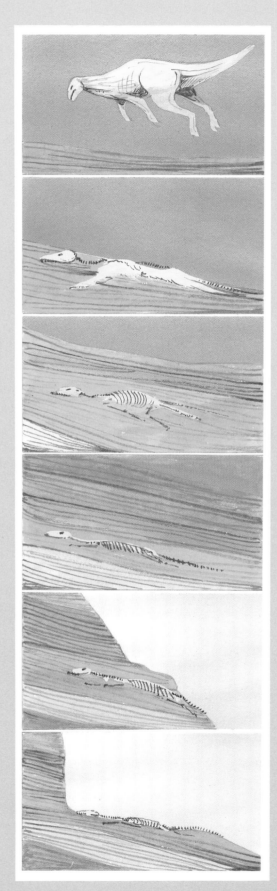

1 A dead dinosaur sinks to the bottom of a lake, river or sea.

2 The skeleton is exposed as the flesh decays. Silt starts to build up.

3 Skeleton now completely covered by layers of silt.

4 The weight of the many layers of silt pressing on the lower layers turns them into rocks.

5 Millions of years later, movements of the Earth's crust expose the bones. Some roll down the hillside.

6 Experts find the bones and dig away the top layers to reveal the bones of the dinosaur.

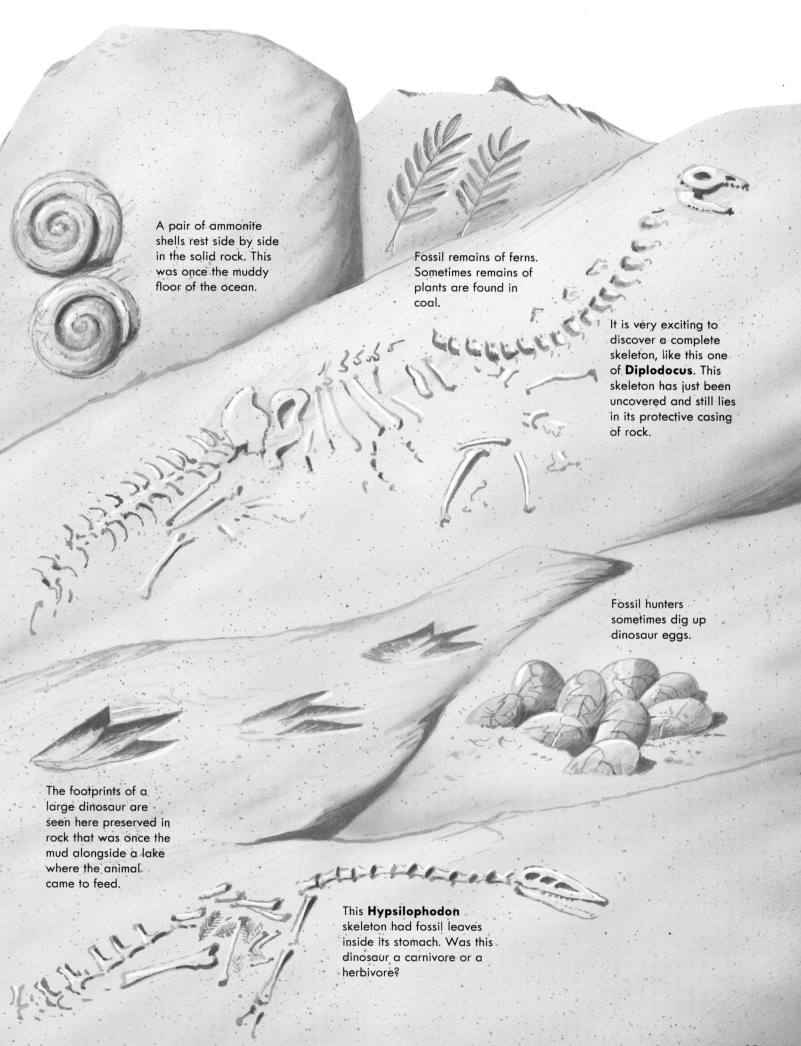

A pair of ammonite shells rest side by side in the solid rock. This was once the muddy floor of the ocean.

Fossil remains of ferns. Sometimes remains of plants are found in coal.

It is very exciting to discover a complete skeleton, like this one of **Diplodocus**. This skeleton has just been uncovered and still lies in its protective casing of rock.

Fossil hunters sometimes dig up dinosaur eggs.

The footprints of a large dinosaur are seen here preserved in rock that was once the mud alongside a lake where the animal came to feed.

This **Hypsilophodon** skeleton had fossil leaves inside its stomach. Was this dinosaur a carnivore or a herbivore?